Six Mini Horses on a Farm

WRITTEN BY: PEGGY SUE LACROIX

Print information available on the last page

Rev. date: 04/23/2015

To order additional copies of this book, contact:
Xlibris
1-888-795-4274
www.Xlibris.com
Orders@Xlibris.com

Six Mini Horses on a Farm

Written By: Peggy Sue LaCroix

Once upon a time, there was three mini horses that lived on a farm with Jack Robbins on a one hundred acre farm, In Portland, Tennessee with His mini horses: Rocky is chocolate and cream, Foxy is all white and thinks she's a classy lady, Pebbles is brown and white pinto and stand up to her brother because they usually disagree when Rocky is in the wrong!! She fights for what she believes in. Farmer Robbins loved his animals, but was really proud of his mini horses!!!

Farmer Robbins

He was out feeding, his horses and other animals one day, When he seen an old friend, another farmer, Hello!!Clancy Cameron!! Said Jack Robbins, "What brings you here today? "Well Jack! Said Clancy, I'm getting old and it's hard for me to take care of my mini horses anymore, "I'd like to ask you if you'd want to give my little horses a good future, So I've come to ask you if you'd take mine!! "Because I'm sick!! And I know you love all your animals And I can't rest until I know they'll be taken care of! "Well of course! "I'd loved to have them here!!Said Farmer Robbins;

Farmer Cameron

Soon Rocky started listening and over heard what was being said; He ran over to Pebbles and Foxy and said; "Looks like we're going to have company around here!!!" And I'm not happy about it!!! "Why? Said Foxy; "sounds like fun!! "Yes!" New friends said; Pebbles!!!! Foxy said; well we'll see how that works out!!! Who knows where they came from!!!! That might change everything around here! And off they went to eat some grass!!!

Suddenly a Horse trailer pulls in to the farm, farmer Clancy Cameron delivering the mini horses! Mr. Robbins and farmer Cameron shook each other hand!! Then Mr. Robbins introduces the other minis to the whole gang, now there are six of you little cuties!!!!Said Mr. Robbins; I would like Rocky and Foxy and Pebbles to come and greet Lilly!! She's a beautiful black and white pinto and Sophia a beautiful blonde and Cody is black and white pinto with a white blaze on his face. Foxy whinnied with excitement!! Wow! I can't wait!!!Pebbles ran to greet them!!

Rocky stood back with an attitude! 'I'll not speak to someone invading my space!" Oh no!! As Rocky stood on his back legs!

Farmer Cameron said; "are you sure they'll be alright here? Farmer Robbins said; Oh yah!!! Rocky's just trying to be a tough guy!!!! They will adjust to one another!! "Okay then" said; Farmer Cameron, "I hope they bring you great pleasure as they did me for so many years!!!!" "Thank you!" Said; Farmer Robbins, I will surely enjoy having them here!!!

As Farmer Robbins opens the bale of hay, Rocky looks and speaks! "You're not eating my hay!!" Pebbles said; "that's not nice!!" You stop! You're being a bully!!Foxy said; "let's try to get to know them first!!!"

Rocky refuses to listen! While Cody tried to eat the hay, Rocky kicked him in the rear! Sophie, Cody's sister got scared! She ran over to her Mother Lilly, "What! "Are we going to do?" Sophie said, "And why are we here?"

"I don't understand this either!!" Lilly said; "but we have to give this place a chance!" We have no place to go!!! I don't understand why? Farmer Cameron didn't want us anymore!!! "We loved him!" Sophie said; "I know I loved him too!!!" The very next day Foxy and Pebbles were getting along with Lilly and Sophie so good, they were racing around the round hay bales.

When Rocky sneaks up and bites Cody in the leg!!!Farmer Robbins, seen him being hateful!!!! It was time to give Rocky a little talking to!!!! And called Rocky to the barn! "You can't be a bully here Rocky!!!!" "I gave my word to farmer Cameron to take special care of his minis!!" Mr. Cameron loved them and I'm sure they loved him too!!! They probably miss there old farm as much as you dislike them here!!! Farmer Robbins scolds him and sends him back out!!! Lilly and Sophie wondering what he'd do next, as he whinnies out to the pasture as if he'd got away with being mean!!! Foxy telling her Dad Rocky "they are very nice, this isn't like you!!! Rocky said; I'm the king around here!! Pebbles and Foxy wasn't going to stand for him being bad anymore!!! Being a bully is wrong!!!

They both went over and talked to Cody's Mom and told her how truly sorry they were for what Rocky had done: Lilly said; "He's going to be sorry one day because one day someone is going to hurt someone he loves!" Then Rocky came charging at them and said; "you don't belong here!!!" Lilly and Sophie were crying!!! Cody comes to their rescue! When Rocky starts to fight with Cody!! The fence got broken from Rocky's back hoof! Out comes Farmer Robbins!! "What's going on out here" he said; Rocky says your new Colt Cody broke the fence!!!!!

Well Mr. Robbins takes Cody to a stall, and says "I'm sorry but this is your time out Cody you'll have to stay here until I have time to fix the fence!!! "But Sir! Said Cody; 'I didn't do it!!!'" Mr. Robbins said; I'll have no fighting here! But Sir Cody said; you don't understand!! Mr. Robbins said; I understand I have to fix my fence!!! And you need to find a way for you and Rocky to get along!!!! You, just stay in that stall and eat for now!!

So while Mr. Robbins was fixing the fence, out in the pasture Lilly, Cody's Mom was worried about her son! She whinnied out of fear! Foxy tried to consul her that Mr. Robbins is a nice man and would never hurt her baby. Meanwhile, Pebbles and Sophie were giving Rocky a lecture, "you did this!" Not Cody!!! "You need to say you're sorry to him!!!!" Rocky looked and smiled yah right!!!!!

Well soon the fence was fixed Cody was back out with the rest of them!! Lilly went to talk to Rocky, to let him know she loves her son and didn't appreciate how he was treating him! Then she galloped off and left him there to think, what he was doing was wrong. Then the others were all having fun running around barrels, but not Rocky. He found out by distancing himself and being angry is no fun!!!

Just when Rocky was ready to give in and say he was sorry! Suddenly, his foot slipped and he fell into the pond, and he couldn't get out!!!! Foxy ran over to him and tried to pull him out by his harness, Pebbles whinnied for help!! Lilly said, I think he's broke his front leg!! Sophie says! "See if you do mean thing, bad things will happen to you! And walked away, well that only left Cody to help!!

He looked at Rocky and said; "let's make a deal" I'll get you out of there, if you agree, we can try to become friends and share this space without anyone getting hurt!!! And we think about others feelings, and show kindness!!!! Rocky said; "Come on then!" "What are you waiting for?" Tell me you're sorry, said Cody!! "Okay" I'm sorry! "Now give me your tail and pull me out of this pond!!!!" Promise you won't bite it! Cody said; "yes!!" I promise said Rocky!!! So Cody tugged and he tugged and out Rocky came!!!!!! Rocky thanked Cody and told him if you agree we can disagree but still try to be friends and share this farm and he was sorry!

Plus Rocky told Cody he had heard Farmer Cameron, said he loved all of you but was just too sick to take care of you all anymore!!! The girls; Pebbles and Foxy, Lilly and Sophie did rare up with joy!! As they finally seen Rocky and Cody become friends!!! They jumped with joy, all but Rocky got up with a limp, but it was only sprained. Mr. Robbins bandaged his ankle!!!!

A month later, Farmer Cameron came to visit and couldn't believe how well they were all getting along!! He greeted them all with a smile and a tear that rolled down his cheek, because is surly loved his mini's. Rocky's leg had healed, and he Cody became best friends! Foxy and Pebbles was happy to play with Sophie and Lilly. A beautiful farm with happy mini horses!!!!! Mr. Robbins told his Mini's every day is a miracle and we must make the best of every day of our life!! Because there's some that aren't as fortunate as you!!!

So love one another with kindness!!!! "We don't need a world of unfairness and sadness!!!" "And I like the way you're all getting along" "I'm so proud of you all!' You're all a part of my family!!See some times change can be quite beautiful!! And they became a happy Mini Horse family!! Farmer Robbins loves his Mini's, Farmer Cameron would check in on them every now and then and say hello!

Cody and Rocky now play together!

Six mini horses Happy on the farm

Foxy is enjoying her new family!

Pebbles, is so proud of her brother now!!

Lilly and Pebbles play together!!!

Life is now peaceful on the Farm!

Sophie enjoys her sunny days! She finely feels at home here! Now they all live happily ever after here on the farm.

THE END

I dedicate this book to the Farmers and families in your home towns, Teachers and hard workers taking care of their animals and family's! Where we honor life with love and care!! May the children enjoy this story, to help stop bullying all over America!

The lesson for our six mini horses

They had to make the best of change, that's part of life! It's easier to get a
long and a lot more fun, they could all be happy if they shared.
Being a bully isn't nice! And no one has fun being bullied around
and it hurts!
Life is more fun if you try to use love and understanding rather than hate.
Makes our world a better place!!! :)
Be kind and understanding, it's a big world, give others their space.
And they'll welcome you with a smile;
Maybe they'll bring joy for a little while,
Everyone is unique and has their own style
With kindness we can live a better life.

Author Biography:

Hello world I'm Peggy Sue LaCroix, I was born in Owosso Michigan September 30, 1958 and I have been writing since 1980, songs and poetry and now I'm opening a new chapter!

Hope you enjoy Six Mini Horses on a Farm.

God has given me a gift in life to always see the beauty of change.

When one door shuts another door opens to a new vision of wonder.

So always be kind to others, you never know how a smile or a kind word will make a difference in someone's day.

Printed in the United States
By Bookmasters